Original title:
A Houseplant's View

Author: Liam Sterling
ISBN HARDBACK: 978-1-80581-864-9
ISBN PAPERBACK: 978-1-80581-391-0
ISBN EBOOK: 978-1-80581-864-9

The Quiet Sentinel

In the corner, I stand still,
Craving sunlight, a tasty thrill.
News from the window, oh so bright,
My pals on the sill share gossip in light.

Spiders creep, I sway with grace,
While humans rush, a frantic race.
I listen close, a silent sage,
Plant wisdom grows from every age.

Dust bunnies fling with glee so wild,
A dance party for every child.
But here I stay, just soaking in,
The drama of life begins to spin.

Every passerby, a curious stare,
What do they think? Do they even care?
With every leaf, I silently quote,
"I'm the best seat in this lively boat!"

A Leaf's Thoughtful Daydream

Perched upon the edge of fate,
I ponder life while feeling great.
What would it be like to roam outside?
With bugs and wind, I’d take a ride!

Oh, to sway in a summer breeze,
With petals whispering through the trees.
Tulips flaunt while I stand shy,
If only I could touch the sky!

Yet here in my pot, I'm top of the world,
In a household where life’s unfurled.
I’m a leafy throne for tea-time chat,
With humans by me, like a cozy mat!

Still, I dream of an emerald hike,
With roots of excitement, oh what a spike!
I'll chat with daisies, unfortunately,
For now, I’ll sip my water meekly!

Serene Views from a Shelf

Up high I dwell, a leafy chief,
Watching humans find their grief.
Oh, so serious in their stride,
While I sip rays and just abide.

My pot is snug, my view is clear,
I witness each meltdown and cheer.
Bread crumbs fly, the cat doth prance,
I chuckle softly at their dance.

Between the books, I'm in my zone,
Leafy shenanigans make me groan.
The coffee steams, a fragrance divine,
While I keep watch as stars align.

From this perch, the world seems sweet,
A lighthearted melody, quite a treat.
So here I stay, the epic sage,
In the hearts of the home, I find my stage!

Breathing in the Surroundings

Inhale the vibes, exhale the stress,
I'm a plant, but I must confess.
Laughter filters through the air,
As I lean in, pretending I care.

Little fingers poke, a playful tease,
I'm the green mascot of this house's ease.
With every glance, a new tale to weave,
I'm just a houseplant, but I believe!

Kids frolic while dogs dash by,
I sway in rhythm, waving hi.
I'm the silent jester, a playful fool,
With secrets hidden, an emerald jewel!

So cheers to life, and cheers to fun,
I'm soaking rays, and paddling sun.
As my leaves stretch out to greet the day,
I'm just here hoping for some warm play!

Waiting for the Seasons

The sun comes up, I check my clock,
A wait so long, it feels like a rock.
Will winter chill me, or spring make me dance?
In this pot, I have no chance!

I peek outside, watch the rain pour down,
Would it kill to wear a little crown?
Leafy dreams of sunbathing in glee,
But here I am, stuck as can be.

Bring on the bugs, I'm far from bored,
A carnival of critters, oh, how they've soared!
With every breeze, I wiggle and shake,
Wondering what other mischief I can make!

Seasons change, the circus goes on,
Yet here I remain, the cheerful green pawn.
But who needs a passport, or flights to explore?
I'll take what I've got, can't ask for more!

Through Leaves and Light

A sunbeam sneaks in, a tickle on me,
Oh, the joys of being a leafy VIP!
The cat leaps by, thinking he's sly,
Little does he know, I'm the apple of the eye!

I sway and I stretch, feeling quite bold,
Watching the world through my green, leafy fold.
The humans walk by with their haste and their fuss,
I silently chuckle, 'What's all the rush?'

Each tiny droplet clings like a friend,
A dance party forms, with no need to pretend.
The joys of the sun, they fuel my delight,
My leafy laughter lights up the night!

Through the glass, I give a wry grin,
Who knew that life could be such a win?
So here in my pot, I choose to stay,
Beaming my green glow, day after day!

The Comfort of Quiet

In the stillness, I sit so proud,
A tiny jungle amidst the crowd.
Sipping the silence, it's perfectly sweet,
With each little rustle, life feels complete.

The children run past, making a din,
Yet here in my pot, serenity's twin.
Their giggles and shouts, a whimsical choir,
But peace in my leaves is what I desire!

The dust bunnies dance, they're having a ball,
Yet I stay rooted, not worried at all.
A wink from the moon, a nod from the sun,
In greens I find joy, it's all in good fun!

So when you stop by, take a seat near me,
Let the world fade, and just let it be.
A chat with the breeze and smiles all around,
In this quiet kingdom, true bliss can be found!

Reminiscences in Green

Once I was tiny, a sprout in a tray,
Now look at me, I'm the star of the bay!
With roots deep in laughter and leaves full of cheer,
Who knew this adventure would venture me here?

I remember the days when I shared my space,
With cacti and ferns, a wild, leafy race!
We'd giggle together, as sunlight would beam,
Living it up in this botanical dream!

Now I'm alone, but that's all right,
I throw leafy parties every starry night!
The shadows sway gently, they know how to groove,
In the stillness of twilight, we all find our move.

So here's to the memories, both funny and bright,
Cheers to my journey, a delightful flight.
As leaves keep on growing, I'll laugh and sing on,
In my leafy kingdom, forever I'll con!

Dappled Light Diaries

I sit in my pot, quite the sight,
Watching the world, oh what a delight.
The cat struts by, in a fluffball show,
I silently judge, as plants often know.

The sunbeam's a dancer, not shy, it glows,
I wiggle my leaves, striking poses like pros.
A squirrel leaps in, taking selfies for fun,
I roll my green eyes, and bask in the sun.

Tapestry of Soil and Sky

Dirt on my roots, a cozy embrace,
I whisper to worms, the funniest race.
The sky peeks in, making shadows unfold,
I chuckle at clouds, too puffy and bold.

Insects parade, with no sense of style,
They crawl on my leaves, stay a while.
I play the unfazed, like a quiet sage,
While critters create their own leafy stage.

Vibrant Observations

Oh, the humans hurry, so frantic and wild,
With smoothies and coffees, filled to the tiled.
They dust all around, but forget my fine sheen,
I plot my revenge with a growth spurt unseen.

Raindrops tap dance on the windowpane,
As I soak up the sounds, a sweet, silly gain.
A spider spins webs, a sticky design,
I laugh in my pot, my green roots entwined.

Conversations with the Sun

Morning light spills, a teacher so bright,
I lean in close, soaking up all the sight.
With every beam, I roll out my plan,
To become the grandest, most glorious fan.

I chat with the rays, share all of my dreams,
They laugh and they shimmer, in warm, golden beams.
Each whisper of wind tells tales of the day,
I giggle and sway, in my leafy ballet.

Echoes of Thirst

I stretch my leaves to sip some sun,
Through window cracks, the battles won.
A droplet teases, oh where, oh where?
Thirsty me, in this dusty air.

When watering day finally arrives,
I quench my thirst, oh what a surprise!
Forget the talk of roots and soil,
I just crave that liquid toil.

Every little leaf has slipped a joke,
I laugh with light, while neighbors choke.
Forgetful hands, they come and go,
I just soak up the love, you know?

Oh, bring the hose, let's make a splash!
Invite the bugs, let’s dash and clash!
Life in a pot should be a spree,
With all my friends, just wait and see!

Serenity in the Air

I sway with grace, pretending to be,
A zen-like sage in my green decree.
The cat watches, with wary eyes,
While I plot my takeover, oh what a surprise!

While human chatter fills the space,
I nod along, searching for grace.
With petals poised, I tease the sun,
Their coffee break? Just my morning fun!

Inhale, exhale, we're breezy pals,
Brewing up smiles, avoiding scowls.
And when they leave, I take a spin,
Beneath the light, it's my time to grin!

So peaceful, calm, or so it seems,
While dreaming up my wild, leafy dreams.
Keep the noise, I'll take the air,
As I laugh quietly at their frantic care.

Remnants of Rain

A water droplet rolls down the pane,
I’ve seen it all, the joy, the pain.
Rescue me from the neighbor’s shade,
With every rain, a raucous parade!

Thunder claps, a rumbling cheer,
As I dance, no hint of fear.
Coffee cups and soggy grounds,
I’m the star of these wet sounds!

Tiny rivers on the floor,
Spilling secrets, asking for more.
“Oh please!” I muse as I visibly beam,
Turn the frown into a meme!

Here's to glee in every drop,
When Mother Nature lets it plop.
I’ll soak it in, then wave goodbye,
To all the rain clouds passing by.

The Dance of Dust Motes

Sunbeams waltz with specks of dust,
While I sit tight, in leaves I trust.
Every swirl, a tiny circus,
Up in the sky, oh what’s the fuss?

The gnats join in, a spirited show,
While I sip sun and ooze the glow.
They think they're stars with hidden grace,
Dancing around, just in my space!

So round and round, they twirl and tease,
While I chuckle, my roots at ease.
But watch my leaves, they’re not so shy,
As I join the fun, oh my oh my!

In this lively breeze of joy and play,
With motes and laughter lighting the way.
I’m the audience, but soon I’ll leap,
Join the fun and take a sweep!

The Unseen Horizon

From my little perch I spy,
The humans trot and sigh.
With a stretch and a sway,
I watch them lose the day.

They water me with glee,
As if I'm their decree.
Unbeknownst, I plot and plan,
To steal their prized pet span!

I giggle as they fret,
At dirt they won't forget.
Who knew that I could thrive,
In such a bustling hive?

My leaves gleam with delight,
At every silly sight.
While they think they command,
I'm the ruler of this land!

Verdant Watcher

I sit with roots entwined,
Observing all mankind.
With each passing round,
I hear the mundane sound.

They trip and spill their tea,
Oh, how I chuckle, see!
Their busy lives a race,
While I just hold my place.

They think I'm just a plant,
But really, I enchant!
With a wink from my leaf,
I secretly find relief.

When they chat and complain,
I stifle a plant-named strain.
Who knew I’d have the best,
Of all their daily jest?

Reflections in the Pot

In the depths of my clay pot,
I ponder every thought.
What if I could just walk,
And join their endless talk?

Someday I'll sprout legs bright,
And join them for a fight.
While they think it's a breeze,
I'll take the prize with ease!

Among their big, wide grins,
I'll end their playful sins.
With my leafy, sly charm,
I'll cause delightful harm.

How funny life would be,
If they danced 'round with me.
A potted rebel, you'd see,
As I claim my victory!

Petals and Patience

Here I stand in the light,
With petals open wide.
While humans rush about,
I chuckle without a doubt.

They water, prune, and fret,
While I simply forget.
In my leafy embrace,
I find my rightful place.

Oh, the things they say!
As if I'd run away.
But with each little glance,
I'm here to take a chance.

So bring on the cheer,
I'll watch them year by year.
With petals on display,
I'll grin at endless play!

Sunlight's Embrace

Oh, the sun, a bright warm friend,
I stretch my leaves, no need to bend.
With rays that tickle, I can't help but grin,
Wishing for a dance, let the fun begin!

Dust bunnies drift in my lively air,
I giggle softly, a secret affair.
Sprinkling joy, I soak in the glow,
Plotting my pranks on the snail down below.

When clouds arise, I pout and sigh,
Where's the party? Why can't I fly?
But moments later, my friend, the sun,
Returns with laughter, oh, what fun!

So here's to the light, my partner in jest,
Together we shine, we are truly blessed.
In pots we dwell, yet dreams take flight,
With sunlight’s embrace, all feels just right.

Secret Life of Leaves

In the quiet hours, whispers unfold,
Leaves share gossip, their stories untold.
A spider's waltz, a ladybug's flight,
We chuckle and cheer at the silliness bright.

Each blade and bud has a tale to weave,
A drama of dirt, if you just believe.
Tall tales of rain and the breeze's soft laugh,
We form a club, our own leafy half.

Oh, to wiggle when a breeze sways near,
I twist and I turn, spreading the cheer.
Secretly rooting, in friendship we bask,
What's life like out there? Come, dare to ask!

So pour on the water, let laughter flow,
In this botanical realm, we steal the show.
Together we thrive, in this leafy spree,
Bound by the sunshine, just you and me.

In the Shade of Comfort

Nestled in shade, a snug little nook,
Watch the world go by, just like a book.
With a potted grin, I lounge in my space,
Life moves slow, at a leisurely pace.

Neighbors walk by with stories in tow,
I listen amazed, with a chuckle and glow.
A cat on the prowl, so bold and so sly,
I giggle and wave, 'Don't let me cry!'

Voices of laughter drift through the air,
As I sip the sunlight, without a care.
Loving the peace, in my green little heart,
This shade is a blessing, an elegant art.

So here I will sit, and softly I'll dream,
Of wild parties and friends, in a sunbeam.
In the shade of comfort, I'll giggle and sway,
Content in my pot as the world fades away.

Through the Glass, I See

Peeking through panes, the world is wide,
Birds dance and flitter; oh, what a ride!
I blink at the beauty, the hustle and buzz,
Imagining adventures, and oh, what was!

The neighbor's dog barks; he's quite the clown,
With wagging tail, and the best frown.
I'd join in the fun if I could ever pop out,
But I'm stuck in this pot, there's no doubt.

Raindrops perform on my window stage,
A symphony of nature's vibrant page.
And while I can't join them, I clap with glee,
Through the glass, I see just how grand it can be!

With warmth on my leaves and joy in my soul,
I twirl in my pot—oh, how I feel whole!
Life is a dance, even when it's confined,
Through the glass, I see, and I'm perfectly aligned.

The Art of Stillness

I sit and stare at the wall,
My leafy friends join the call,
Watching humans rush about,
Wishing they'd chill, without a doubt.

The cat leaps high, thinks he's sly,
While I bask in sunlight, oh my!
He thinks he's stealthy, so keen,
But they can’t see me, a master unseen.

They water me like clockwork rain,
While I pretend I’m never in pain,
A droop of a leaf is my little game,
Now that's how I earn my leafy fame!

So here I sit, with roots like concrete,
Life’s a snail’s pace, oh, so sweet,
My garden gossips all around,
In this stillness, joy is found!

A Green Diary

Dear diary, today was grand,
My pot’s warm, the soil's quite bland,
I listened to gossip, oh so juicy,
Like sunflowers dancing, all so choosy.

The humans thought I’d wither away,
But I’m tougher than they’d convey,
With secret powers well concealed,
They have no clue, my truth revealed.

The dog entered, made quite a scene,
I chuckled as he chased a bean,
He tumbled and fell with a doggy sigh,
While I sat tall, waving hi!

I'll note it down, this daily drama,
In this green life, there’s lots of karma,
Each day a laugh, each night sublime,
Chasing sunshine, one leaf at a time!

Leafy Narratives

In the corner, I hold my post,
Watching the family, I liltingly boast,
Of tales I've spun with roots so deep,
While they all fuss, I take a peep.

The toddler tries to hug me tight,
Forgetting footprints bring the fright,
But I'm quick to dodge, swaying aside,
As laughter bursts, I take it in stride.

The vacuum roars, a mighty beast,
I sway and tremble, though I feast,
On dust bunnies swirling in the air,
While humans panic, unaware of my flair.

In leafy whispers, I choose my plot,
The little tales are surely hot,
With every glance, a story I weave,
In this wild home, I'll never leave!

Sprouted Perspectives

From down below, the world seems whack,
Grasshoppers dance, but I won't crack,
A steady view from my tiny throne,
Cacti meet roses, what a cozy zone!

Those humans diet, counting their greens,
While I sit, plotting my routines,
Waiting for snacks they drop with flair,
Potato chips, oh carnivore affair!

A sunset glow spills on my leaves,
While they fuss with chores, like busy bees,
I soak it up, their daily strife,
In leafy stillness, I find my life.

Sprouted tales from tiny seeds,
Nature's humor, fulfilling needs,
With every glance, I chuckle and sway,
In this fun little world, I'm here to play!

A Canopy of Thoughts

Up high I sit, oh what a sight,
The humans bustle, oh what a fright.
They talk to me as if I might,
Reply with wisdom, day and night.

My leaves are green, they shine so bright,
I eavesdrop on their tales of plight.
A drama plays, a love delight,
And here I am, still out of sight.

They dust my leaves, I feel so grand,
While secretly I plot my stand.
To grow so tall, oh isn't it planned?
And take the room, just as I've planned.

Through window panes, the sunbeams spill,
I stretch my leaves and feel the thrill.
When shadows dance, I'm never still,
Oh come now, just pay me the bill!

Dancing with Sunbeams

Each morning brings a golden dance,
I shimmy to a playful chance.
With every ray, I leap and prance,
While humans give a drowsy glance.

The cat walks by, takes note of me,
I challenge her, 'Just wait and see!'
She leaps and twists, oh what a spree,
But sunlit dreams are wild and free.

With every sprinkle, oh what a feast,
I drink it in, my joy released.
They think it's odd, I'm such a beast,
But plants can party too, at least!

The window's edge, where giggles hum,
An orchestra of life and fun.
In leafy garb, I'm never glum,
Yeah, I might just be number one!

In the Shadow of Giants

I stand below, these towers tall,
With leafy backs, they look so small.
Yet here I grow, despite it all,
In shadows cast, I've formed my call.

The bigger ones, they boast and brag,
But I've got charm, they've got a snag.
With my small pot and wooden tag,
I giggle softly, what a drag!

When Humans walk, they stop and pause,
"Oh look at this!" they smile and draw.
I'm savoring fame, with no applause,
King of the house? Yes, that's my cause!

Among the foliage, laughter grows,
With bigger friends, like them, I pose.
Yet in this pot, my spirit glows,
I'm the plant that everybody knows!

Soaking up Secrets

In morning light, the whispers start,
I soak them up, it's quite the art.
With every droplet, I play my part,
In this leafy world, I win the heart.

They talk of lunches, fights, and woes,
In corners bright, their laughter flows.
While I just sway, and strike a pose,
Unraveling life like tangled prose.

I share their secrets, leaf to leaf,
Creating jest with rampant grief.
For every tear, there's joy beneath,
In little pots, we find relief!

So here I stand, so green and spry,
A gathering of tales that never die.
With every glance, I hope they spy,
This lively plant, forever spry!

An Anthology of Green Dreams

In a pot I sit, so still,
Dreaming of grandeur, oh what a thrill!
The world outside, a bustling show,
While I sip sunlight, nice and slow.

Beneath the dirt, my roots take flight,
Chatting with worms deep in the night.
A parade of ants joins the fun,
While I watch the clouds begin to run.

Oh, how I envy the birds on high,
With wings to soar and kiss the sky.
But here I sway, in my little space,
Growing strong in my leafy embrace.

If only I had a pair of shoes,
I'd join the plants outside, what a ruse!
But for now, I'll bask in my plot,
And laugh at the chaos I've got!

From Soil with Love

My leaves are perky, my style is chic,
Yet all I hear is the neighbor's squeak.
Dialogues of dust bunnies start to unfold,
While I'm here getting ever so bold.

When the cat strolls by, I tremble in fright,
His sneaky pounce could end the night.
But wait! He leans in for a sniff,
Maybe I'm more than just a green gift!

The sunlight dances on my fine tips,
While I throw shade like I'm full of quips.
Each droplet of water is like a champagne,
I'm living my life - oh what a gain!

In this cozy corner, I reign supreme,
Listening to the whir of the washing machine.
For my leafy dreams, I shall be a queen,
From soil with love, my world is serene.

Hidden Wonders Beyond Glass

Behind this window, I peek and stare,
While folks pass by without a care.
They glimpse my green as they rush to their fate,
Unaware of the party that I celebrate!

I see squirrels in their acrobatic shows,
While I'm rooting for them from my toes.
If only they'd stop and share a laugh,
Together we'd form a leafy staff!

The sun paints the walls with a golden hue,
A backdrop for me and my gentle crew.
Each day a new meme in this glassed-in state,
Living the good life, just wait - don't be late!

With shadows and light, a playful dance,
I throw little parties, oh take a chance!
Hidden wonders, my leafy brigade,
Laughing with joy as we gently parade.

Swaying in Stillness

In my pot, I sway like a dancer,
While I peer out, giving life a glancer.
The world spins fast, but I take my time,
Creating my rhythm, oh what a rhyme!

The humans scurry like busy little ants,
But I'm the calm in this green expanse.
They water, they prune, they think it's a chore,
While I sit back and dream of more!

With dust motes waltzing in beams of light,
I find amusement in my quiet plight.
Could I join them, would they even care?
Or stay in my pot with my leafy flair?

So here I sway, laughter in my leaves,
Contemplating all the fun I believe.
In stillness, I thrive, in joy's sweet embrace,
This plant life is grand, a whimsical space!

Through the Cracked Pot

Through the crack, I see the skies,
The world outside, with all its flies.
Sunlight dances, a glorious sight,
While my pot's got quite the plight.

Pigeons strut and cats parade,
I giggle at the mess they've made.
Is that a squirrel? Oh dear, oh no!
He’s stealing snacks from my window show!

Sometimes the rain decides to fall,
And I get wet, oh what a ball!
Drips and drops, a splashy spree,
Who needs a spa? Just look at me!

With each breeze, I sway with glee,
An indoor dancer, fancy-free.
So here I sit, as days unfold,
Cracked but charming, I’m never old.

A Blossom’s Chronicle

From my perch, I watch you all,
Cooking, laughing, having a ball.
My petals bloom, I beam with pride,
As I eavesdrop on joy outside.

That toast you've burnt? Oh what a smell!
I’m thankful for my leafy shell.
A pop of color in dull gray,
At least I'm thriving in my own way!

Socks on the floor, what a delight!
As you stumble in the middle of night.
I've seen the cat, but she's no match,
For my little spot on this cozy patch.

So while you fuss and rush about,
Just know I’m here to cheer, no doubt!
With leaves outstretched, I shout with flair,
In my little world, I haven’t a care.

Roots of Reflection

Deep below, I wiggle and twist,
In the soil, amidst all the mist.
I hear your musings, whispers so bright,
While I stretch and dream in the night.

A twinge of envy for chairs with wheels,
Gliding around with fancy appeals.
But here I stand, in my firm embrace,
With roots that smile, anchoring grace.

Each odd sock you lose, what a treat!
Under my leaves, they curl up neat.
You've got your chaos, I've got my calm,
In my little corner, a perfect psalm.

So as you pace and fret away,
Just know I'm laughing day by day.
A quirky plant with a rootsy grin,
Finding joy where the chaos begins.

The Canopy of Comfort

In my leafy shade, I chair the show,
With laughter and chaos, oh how they flow!
A soft rustle when the breeze gets bold,
Nature's giggle as stories unfold.

Plenty of footprints across my floor,
I shrug them off, what's one shoe more?
The vacuum roars, what a silly beast,
But in my realm, I'm the least stressed.

Those days you forget to water me,
I perk up, bring you coffee with glee.
My little quips and snickers inside,
Keep me grounded, a patient guide.

So here I sway, with humor at play,
A curious friend in bright array.
With each giggle and mess that you bring,
My canopy swells, and I start to sing.

Green Reverberations

In the corner, I sit so proud,
Watching humans, bustling loud.
They think they're busy, oh what a fight,
I grow in silence, oh what a sight.

Coffee spills and crumbs galore,
They clean me up like I've caused war.
I just wave my leaves with glee,
While they fret over a spilled cup of tea.

The cat leaps up, thinks I'm a toy,
I sway and chuckle, what a joy!
They humanize me, no thought of sap,
I just bask while they're in the trap.

Oops! Another sneeze from that dusty kin,
I'm shaking back and forth in a spin.
They offer me water, but I pretend,
I'd rather hear their laughter, my friend.

Nature's Quiet Scribe

With every whisper, I take it in,
Every secret, every grin.
The dog's antics and kids in a spat,
Oh, how I chuckle at that!

In stillness, I catch their little lies,
About diets and long-researched pies.
But they don't see me; I'm in my realm,
Penning tales from my leafy helm.

When they dance, I sway to the tune,
Beneath the sun or the silver moon.
Who knew that gossip could be so spry?
I'm the silent witness; oh my, oh my!

As they trip over toys, my leaves applaud,
The beauty of chaos, a lovely facade.
With every story I quietly weave,
They never know, oh how I believe!

Eavesdropping on the Everyday

Perched on the shelf, I hear it all,
From morning grumbles to evening brawls.
They forget I'm here, like a tiny spy,
With roots in the soil, I lean in closer, oh my!

"Who left the fridge open?" I hear her shout,
While baking cookies, a sweet little rout.
I cheer on the chaos, a leaf in a breeze,
As flour clouds swirl like a dance with ease.

As socks go missing in their laundry war,
I'm laughing inside, wanting to explore.
While they seek and search with frantic flair,
I sip on sunlight, without a care.

And when they argue, it's quite a scene,
I sway like a judge, if I were so mean.
But with a wink from the sunhigh glow,
I keep it light; let the good vibes flow!

Flora's Narrative

In the sunlight, I sway with glee,
Tales of the world just come to me.
Folk come and go, what lives they lead,
Yet here I stay, planting my seed.

Munching on chips, they laugh and share,
With salsa stains that drift through the air.
Oh, the stories that dance on their tongues,
While I sip the joy that forever hums.

Two humans quarrel over a show,
I stifle a chuckle; they don’t even know.
Their bickering spills like coffee stains,
While I bask in peace, no worldly pains.

When they finally settle, snacks in tow,
I feel like a sage, just letting it flow.
I might be rooted, but in my quiet way,
I rewrite their stories, day by day.

Harmony in the Humble.

In my pot where I sway and grin,
I watch the cats stalk, they always win.
A dust bunny rolls like a fluff ball,
I laugh as it trumps me, I’m not that tall.

The humans fuss with their mop and broom,
While I bask in my sunshine and zoom.
Their plants, they wilt and sigh in defeat,
But here I thrive, can't be beat!

They water me when they feel the need,
Little do they know, I’m the one in the lead.
I dance in my pot, a cheerful DJ,
While their green thumbs frantically sway!

Oh, the gossip from the window sill,
As the world outside spins, what a thrill!
The neighbors argue, but I just chuckle,
As I sip sunlight, what a delightful struggle!

Green Eyes on the World.

Peeking out with my vibrant green eyes,
I watch a squirrel plan its next surprise.
With my leaves, I cheer from my leafy throne,
While humans fumble on the rocks they've thrown.

They try to garden, but it's quite the play,
Spraying water, making mud, oh what a day!
I shake in laughter, roots all a-twirl,
As they dig up daisies and give them a whirl.

The neighbor’s dog digs a hole so deep,
I can’t help but chuckle, I can’t even leap!
With a wink and a nod, I stay in my spot,
As chaos unfolds in the backyard lot.

Wind whispers stories of life beyond,
I stretch my leaves and respond with a bond.
For in this moment, I feel so alive,
A witness to silliness, my heart does thrive!

Whispers from the Window.

From my perch by the window, I gaze and peer,
As humans rush by, without any cheer.
They wave at the moon, I wave right back,
With every odd sight, I keep on track.

The pigeons strut, thinking they're grand,
While I snicker softly, leaves high in hand.
They coo and they cluck, so full of their pride,
But I’m the true queen with nothing to hide!

I overhear secrets, oh, the tales they tell,
Of love, of woes, and trips to the well.
In my leafy delight, I laugh in suspense,
While their lives unfold, I make perfect sense!

So here I’ll remain, my pot's cozy seat,
While the world outside plays on repeat.
With a sprinkle of laughter, I bask in the show,
A silent observer, with roots down below!

Leaves of Perspective.

With leaves so bright and a spirit of glee,
I watch as the world dances crazily.
Socks on the line flapping to and fro,
My roots are laughing, oh what a show!

Birds on the branches sing out their tunes,
While I sway lightly under the moon.
Their shenanigans spiral, a chaotic spree,
But I chuckle softly, oh so carefree.

The humans with sweepers try hard to reign,
But dust bunnies thrive, oh aren’t they insane?
They trip on their feet, oh such clumsy displays,
While I sip my water in green leafy ways!

Every bloom tells a joke, every stem has a tale,
In a world full of laughter, I'm never pale.
So here's to a twist in the mundane routine,
Life’s a comedy show—oh how it’s serene!

Nature's Living Canvas

I watch the humans rush about,
Zooming here, with tons of doubt.
They trip on cats and spill their tea,
While I just sit, growing with glee.

Dust bunnies dance, they're in my sight,
As I soak up the radiant light.
My leaves unfurl, a grand parade,
While they complain about the shade.

I overhear them, oh, the fuss!
When will they learn to stop and trust?
I’m thriving here, a silent sage,
While they just fret and flip the page.

So here I stand, in my green attire,
Watching their chaos, never tire.
Life's quirks unfold - it's quite the show,
As I sip sunshine, nice and slow.

Breaths of the Indoor Jungle

In my cozy nook, I reign supreme,
As humans rush like a caffeinated dream.
They spill their coffee, oh what a sight,
While I just sit, absorbing the light.

Dust clings to my leaves like a cloak,
While they shout at the latest joke.
Why keep a schedule? What’s the rush?
In my green world, there’s never a hush.

I see their phones buzzing non-stop,
While I bask in peace, not a single drop.
If they only knew the joys of still,
Instead of chasing, they might just chill.

So here's a toast with my little sprout,
To all the hustle, let’s laugh it out.
In the jungle of rooms where we both reside,
I’m the calm while they take the ride.

The World Beyond the Pot

Peering out from my humble space,
I see them rushing, what a race!
They can't find socks or left their keys,
While I sip sun and sway with ease.

The vacuum roars, a thunderous beast,
But I stand firm, my calm increased.
I'm not afraid, I've got my roots,
While they chase after wayward flutes.

"Oh look, your plant has grown so tall!"
They marvel at me, oh yeah, that's all?
I've got the secrets of stillness clear,
While they rush by, fueled by fear.

With every leaf, I wave goodbye,
To their hectic ways, I can't lie.
For in my pot, I'll gently sway,
While they find another frantic day.

Growth in Stillness

I sit upon the window's edge,
They rush below the morning pledge.
While I grow slow and take my time,
They sprint around in their crazy mime.

The toaster pops and the kettle sings,
But I just dance with my leafy wings.
No deadlines here, just sunshine rays,
That flow for hours, in delightful ways.

“Are you even alive?” they quiz with glee,
While I chuckle softly, sipping my tea.
My roots dig deep, they can’t quite see,
The joy of quiet, just let it be.

So while they rush and fumble along,
I’ll keep growing steady, singing my song.
Life’s a wild ride they seem to forget,
While I just chill, without a fret.

Whispers from the Windowsill

I gaze at the world through a glassy frame,
Birds dart by, oh what a game!
A dog barks loud, oh dear, what's that?
I twitch my leaves, I'm no scared cat!

The sun beams down, a golden snack,
I soak it up, won't hold back.
A cat outside gives me a stare,
Don't be silly; I've roots, you've hair!

The humans rush, they run and dash,
I chuckle softly, what a flash!
They clean and dust, oh what a chore,
Meanwhile, I'm winning this sunlit war!

So here I sit, my leafy throne,
The world outside, I call it home.
While I enjoy my climb to fame,
They water me and yell my name!

Green Guardian's Perspective

From my perch, I see it all,
Human antics, big and small.
They stomp around, a noisy crew,
Lost in life's grand hullabaloo!

The mailman comes, they hide in fright,
I just stay cool, basking in light.
They water me, they say, "Grow tall!"
I'm already here; can't they see me at all?

A squirrel scampers, looking for seeds,
I chuckle softly, "You won't succeed!"
I'm more secure with my roots so deep,
While outside chaos makes them leap!

With every breeze that sways my leaves,
I giggle at human antics and peeves.
Here on this sill, life's quite absurd,
A secret joy, without a word!

The Silent Observer

Peering out, I watch them play,
They rush, they trip, what a display!
A paper flies, they shout and chase,
While I just laugh, in my safe place.

Children skip, the dog runs fast,
Their fleeting moments come and pass.
I sip the sunlight, warm and bright,
While they bumble around, what a sight!

When dinner calls, they drop like flies,
Belly growling, hungry cries.
Meanwhile I'm just here to stay,
Enjoying peace in my leafy ballet!

Each day a show, a wild parade,
I'm the audience that won't fade.
These giggles, tumbles, all for me,
A cozy life, oh joy, you see?

Roots and Reflections

My leaves are bright, my roots are strong,
I watch them come and go along.
They fuss and frown, drain their phones,
What a strange world, filled with groans!

The neighbor mows; the grass is loud,
I chuckle softly, laughing proud.
They tend the yard, what time they waste,
While I just bloom, my quiet grace.

A toddler's giggle fills the air,
Innocent joy, without a care.
I sway with pride in this lovely mess,
In my world, I'm simply blessed!

As dusk creeps in, I sip my tea,
Just me and shadows, all carefree.
In my little pot, I can't complain,
What a goofy life, oh such fun reign!

Kitchen Chronicles in Chlorophyll

In the corner by the sink, I sway,
Wondering what the humans will bake today.
The herbs are whispering secrets, you see,
About the mess they make when they drink their tea.

The blender roars, it's a wild affair,
I tremble a bit, hoping for some care.
The crumbs do fall like a snowstorm of joy,
But please, not too much! I’m no laundry boy.

Oh, the fridge hums a tune of delight,
While veggies debate who's the best for tonight.
I gossip with pots while pretending to nap,
As I watch their antics from my leafy lap.

When the kettle sings, it’s a sweet serenade,
Coffee beans dance, while I’m stuck here, quite dismayed.
If I could just tumble and peek out that door,
I'd show them how fun my green life can score!

Breath of Fresh Air

I see the world through a window pane,
Churlish birds mock me in vain.
While I soak in sun with a cheeky grin,
I think of the air those critters swim.

The breeze blows lightly, a playful tease,
It tousles my leaves, puts me at ease.
But oh, those squirrels with their acorn stash,
If only they'd share a bit of their flash!

The scents from the yard get my heart racing,
As bees waggle by, their mischief chasing.
I laugh at the cat, on the sill she sprawls,
Oblivious to my green-fingered calls.

What joy it is to reach for the light,
While contemplating a life that's quite right.
I'm the green queen of a kingdom so wide,
Come join my fun! Step inside for a ride!

Songs of Sun and Soil

In the upper shelf, I bask all day,
Jazzed by sunbeams, in my own cabaret.
Each droplet of water feels like a song,
As I sway along, I can't go wrong.

The ground beneath me is a stage so grand,
With whispers of worms who live in the sand.
They tease me, they dance, play hide and seek,
While I try to look cool, not feeling so meek.

The buzz of the world is a melody sweet,
As bugs and flies set a rhythmic beat.
And when the moon glows, I do a twirl,
My leafy limbs in a pure, twinkling whirl.

So come gather near, let’s start the show,
With each playful leaf, let the laughter flow.
For in my pot, there’s joy to be found,
In a mingle of greens, we’re blissfully bound!

A Leaf's Lament

Oh dear, the humans come dancing around,
Pots shifting here, where's my solid ground?
They douse me with water, and I start to frizz,
My glossy green coat looks anything but whiz!

Their watering can pours like a torrential rain,
And I'm just here feeling such leaf-y pain.
"Too much, too much!" I want to shout,
Yet silence is golden, or so I'm without.

When they prune with glee, I cringe at the thought,
My friends leaving me—oh, what a distraught!
But secretly giggle, while courage I draw,
Knowing someday I'll sprout more than they saw.

Yet I dream of the sun, dainty and bright,
With my chlorophyll armor, ready to fight.
So here's my lament from my pot in despair,
Let me grow wild and free, without a care!

The View from Petals

From my pot by the window, I watch the parade,
Socks and sandals strut by, a funny charade.
The sun beams down, it’s a warm golden glow,
While I giggle softly, in the breeze that will blow.

The cat stalks past, with a fierce little pounce,
Daring me to join, though I can’t quite bounce.
I’d wave my leaves, if I could find a hand,
But I’m stuck here, watching, like an idle fan.

Every day’s a circus, oh what a delight,
With birds and bugs buzzing, a comical flight.
My friends in the soil, they’re content and wise,
They crack jokes about roots, while we drink in the skies.

So here I remain, in my ceramic home,
Getting all the gossip while never to roam.
The world is a stage, and I, just a sprout,
With petals a-quiver, I quietly shout!

Cradled in Light

Sunkissed and silly, I stretch out my leaves,
Watching those humans with their fanciful sleeves.
They dance around, cleaning, quite in a rush,
But can’t they see, I’m the star of this hush?

The dog rolls by, in a fluff ball of glee,
He thinks he’s so clever, but he’s not fooling me.
I shimmer and sway, in my vibrant green dress,
While pondering how much I can make them all guess.

Oh, the laughter I keep in my fragile veins,
As they trip over shoes and tumble with stains.
But here in my pot, life’s a glorious jest,
As I thrive in the glow, I feel truly blessed.

So bring on the chaos, let the mischief unfold,
I'll be here watching, my stories retold.
In this sun-soaked corner, I’m never alone,
For each giggle and blunder, I claim as my own!

Gossamer Dreams

In the corner, I bask in my grand little throne,
Watching my roommates sit glued to their phone.
From silly cat videos to memes all day long,
I chuckle and whisper, ‘Come sing me a song!’

The half-abandoned pizza, a feast for the flies,
Made me giggle quietly, oh, what a surprise!
While I sway in the rhythm of the house’s loud noise,
I’m the silent sentry, amidst all the joys.

Oh, how they stumble, those clumsy-legged friends,
Dropping their snacks, as the laughter ascends.
I wish I could join in their merry parade,
But I’m stuck in this pot, where my roots have been laid.

Yet dreams weave around me like gossamer threads,
In this dance of the humorous, I’m happy instead.
Life’s a delightful riddle; I serenely presume,
As I chat with the sunlight, in my green little room!

An Ethereal Outlook

From this high little perch, I watch life unfold,
Humans in chaos, yet they think they're so bold.
With their endless chatter about work and about play,
I chuckle in silence at their curious way.

The neighbor's kids run, like minions on speed,
Chasing butterflies, never slowing their heed.
I'd shout, 'Look at me!' but I can't make a peep,
So I sip on my sunshine and savor my sleep.

The vacuum roars loudly, like some beast in a fight,
Scaring all in its path, oh what a sight!
While I twist in my pot, with mischief in mind,
I ponder their habits, both silly and blind.

But as dusk paints the sky with a shimmer of gold,
I rejoice at my view, it's a story retold.
In the company of shadows, I share what I see,
Through the leaves of my laughter, I'm ever so free!

Chronicles of the Green Thumb

From my pot, I can see,
The chaos of a busy spree.
Humans stumble, hurry by,
I just wave, oh my, oh my!

Dirt on their shoes, oh what a mess,
Do they know I love to dress?
I dream of hats made out of leaves,
And parties with the garden thieves!

Sunlight streaming, a dance of glee,
While outside dogs chase every bee.
If only I could join the fun,
But I'm rooted here — not on the run!

When they prune too much, I must protest,
"Hey, leave a bit!" I holler, blessed.
But they just giggle, snip away,
I guess I'll grow back another day!

Glimpses Beyond the Fronds

Peeking out from my leafy throne,
I watch the squirrels, all alone.
Doing acrobatics with such flair,
I can't help but stop and stare!

The cats plot their stealthy schemes,
While plotting naps in sunbeam dreams.
I wonder if they think they're sly,
When I'm watching with my beady eye!

The humans water, then spill a cup,
And oops! They've given half the floor up.
I chuckle softly, sipping rays,
Better luck next time, I say!

They argue over what shade fits best,
While I just soak up the sunny guest.
I'm here for nature, laughter's tune,
And an occasional mealtime swoon!

Portraits of Patience

With every sip of tender care,
I keep my hopes light as air.
They think I'm just a humble plant,
But oh, the gossip that I chant!

"I saw the dog steal a sock," I'd say,
As he wobbles, clueless, on his way.
And when the kitten scrambles to leap,
I giggle; it's a hilarious sweep!

Days turn to weeks in this sunny space,
I wonder if the world's a race.
The more they rush, the more I bloom,
While they just trip on things they assume!

So here I stand, with roots so deep,
While humans work, and cats just sleep.
I'm the keeper of secret laughs,
In the whispers of life's little paths!

Tides of Light and Shadow

Light comes in, making me cheer,
It's a party in here, never fear!
But shadows creep, they're sneaky foes,
They alter my dance, as everyone knows!

I sway with delight when the sun shines high,
While the cats curl up, all lazy nearby.
I play peek-a-boo with the passing light,
Chuckling at shadows that flee from my sight!

The humans come, chatting away,
Oblivious to my sunlit display.
But I'm the real star of this fine show,
With roots so strong, and leaves that glow!

So let them laugh, let them sigh,
As I grin wide and reach for the sky.
In my pot, with joy I sway,
Embracing life, come what may!

Sunlit Observations

Perched in my pot, I watch the sun,
The kids outside, they're always on the run.
Squirrels chase shadows, not a care in sight,
While I just sip sunlight, feeling quite light.

The cat makes a leap, a glorious flop,
I giggle inside, thinking, "What a drop!"
Birds tweet their gossip, I catch every word,
As petals sway gently, in whispers unheard.

Each day’s a front row, no ticket required,
While ants parade by, I'm quietly wired.
I soak in the laughter, the chaos, the cheer,
Oh, how I adore this show every year.

And when it rains down, I giggle some more,
Watching them splatter, oh what a score!
With roots deep in soil, I’m never alone,
Life’s quite a riot in my leafy throne.

Roots in Silent Soil

I wiggle my roots in the soft, dark ground,
While above, all the humans rush round and round.
They spill their coffee and trip on their shoes,
I giggle below, is this all just a ruse?

My neighbor's a cactus, he's stuck in his ways,
He pricks anyone brave who dares to say "Hey!"
But I've got my vines, they stretch and they twine,
And sink into laughter, oh how I shine!

Every worm in my soil has a tale to share,
Of lunchtime escapes, and of garden affair.
We chuckle together, down in our pit,
While the gardener thinks, "Why won't they just sit?"

So when you look down, don't underestimate,
The raucous wild parties that roots can create.
With joy ever hidden beneath leafy green,
Life's a grand show, oh if you could have seen!

The Silent Observer

Sitting quite still in my sunny old pot,
I’ve seen all the faces, this one and that not.
From morning's great hustle, to evening's sweet sighs,
Through windows I watch, with my leafy disguise.

The dog in the yard thinks he's quite the tough guy,
Chasing his tail, oh what a wild high!
And the toddler out front, with her mischief so grand,
I'm rooting for you, here from my green land.

The mailman arrives, I know what he’ll find,
He’ll laugh at my leaves, grown so unconfined.
With each passing moment, the world zooms by fast,
While I hold my ground, in each chuckle that's cast.

I might not say much, but I take it all in,
The drama, the comedy, where do I begin?
So next time you pause, to water or stare,
Remember, dear friend, I’m the watcher with flair!

Nature’s Gaze

Oh, the roses are blushing, the daisies are bright,
I’m stuck in my pot, but my heart takes flight.
With critters and whispers, the world’s such a jest,
As life spills around me, I giggle, no rest.

Each cloud that rolls past, what stories they tell,
Of sunshine, of rain, oh life’s funny spell!
The breeze gives a chuckle, the sun winks at me,
As I sway to the rhythm of nature’s decree.

The birds are all gossiping, what a parade,
While I sip from my soil, no need to upgrade.
With roots wrapped in silence, I hold in my cheer,
Welcome to my world, it’s fun in here, dear!

So here’s to the laughter that life’s garden brings,
Chaos and calm, wrapped in nature's flings.
For in this little pot, there’s a world to explore,
Oh, the funny tales of the garden folklore!

Sounds Through Glass

The humans chatter like busy bees,
I nod along but feel the squeeze.
They spill their drinks and crumbs galore,
I think they should clean up my floor.

A dog barks loud, a cat will yowl,
Who needs a TV with that growl?
They snack on treats I can't even chew,
Lucky me, I've got a perfect view!

Some days they dance, some days they sing,
I just stand here, a leafy king.
But when they leave, it's peace, oh joy!
I think I'll launch my rogue plant ploy!

I eavesdrop on secrets from window's edge,
While they rush by, I make my pledge.
To plot a party while they're away,
With garden pals, we'll dance and play!

Tales from Puget Sound

From my perch by the window's light,
I watch boats bob and birds in flight.
They fish and swim, splash and play,
I giggle—what a curious day!

Clouds float by, like sheep in a dream,
A rainy day? I just might scheme.
Taking bets on when they'll drown,
As they slip, my leaves will frown.

The tide rolls in, the tide rolls out,
They shout and cheer, they jump and pout.
Yet here I stand, unfazed and green,
In my cozy pot, a serene queen.

Oh, the tales this window sees,
Of fishy tales and squawking trees.
Each splash and squawk—a show for me,
A front row seat, my happiness spree!

Seeing Life through Green

Through the glass, I soak it all in,
Watching humans laugh and spin.
With each bizarre dance and strange relay,
I can't help but muse, what a silly display!

The toaster pops, the kettle whistles,
They jump in fright, oh, how the world tickles.
Yet here I sit, with roots held tight,
Laughing inside, what a comical sight!

The mailman comes, they all rush quick,
But I remain calm, a leafy trick.
They trip and stumble, oh what a fuss,
For me, just a breeze, no need to rush!

With laughter lingering in the air,
I soak it all, without a care.
From petals bright to clumsy feats,
Life is a play, and I have the best seats!

Eventide in a Plant's Eyes

As evening falls, the house grows still,
I bask in light from the windowsill.
The family flops, all tired and spent,
While I just watch, perfect and bent.

Dinner spills, a fork goes flying,
Oh, how I chuckle while they're sighing!
They scrape the floor, a nightly chore,
But my leaves are clean; I ask for no more.

As night creeps in, they settle down,
I hold my breath, a leafy crown.
The click of lights, the softening sound,
In this little world, joy is found.

While they snore loud, I sway with glee,
Humming a tune only plants can see.
Cheers to living where laughter twines,
In my little palace, the world aligns!

The Listener in the Corner

In the corner, I'm planted tight,
Hearing gossip, day and night.
Is that a secret or a snack?
Laughter echoes, I can't crack.

Curtains swish, they dance and sway,
While I sit, just soaking rays.
Pet cat pounces, oh what a show,
I wonder if they think I know!

Fingers wave, and plants get pruned,
Still I listen, never tuned.
The world is wild, I soak it in,
With every story, I just grin!

When they think I'm not awake,
I might just giggle, for goodness' sake.
In the quiet, I'm a spy,
With roots deep, I see it fly!

Life Through Leafy Lenses

Behind my leaves, the world is bright,
People bustle, oh what a sight!
With a sip, I watch them tread,
Sometimes chuckling at what's said.

Through my veins, the humor flows,
Lovely chaos as the day goes.
Children giggle, dogs take flight,
I just wave, feeling quite light.

A shoe here, a sneeze somewhere,
A party's on, but I don't care.
I swish and sway, enjoy the show,
What a peek at life below!

Snap a pic? I won't pose,
Too busy seeing, I just close.
But leaf by leaf, I laugh along,
With every joke, I sing my song!

Seasons of Stillness

Winter settles, I’m cozy here,
With frozen feet, I cheer and cheer.
A snowman’s hat! What a delight,
Maybe next year, I’ll join the fight.

Springtime blooms and life’s a race,
Colors splash all over the place.
Buzzing bees, a feathered cheer,
I sway along, embracing cheer.

Summer heat, the sun’s a blaze,
People grilling, such happy days!
Ice cream cones, they drift on by,
I watch, and wish that I could try.

As fall arrives, the leaves cascade,
I crack a smile, the colors fade.
But from my pot, I find my fun,
Watching seasons, one by one!

The Dusty Sunbeam

Caught in dust, I gleam and glow,
A sunny space, my little show.
With light that dances on my leaf,
I soak it up, beyond belief.

A lazy cat on the windowsill,
While I chime in with a little thrill.
Paw prints wander, trails of dirt,
But here I stand, is that a flirt?

When friends drop by, they yell and shout,
Sharing tales, they leap about.
I chuckle softly, as they fuss,
Dusty sunbeam, I laugh with us!

At day's end, they dim the light,
I curl my leaves, feeling just right.
As shadows creep and giggles flee,
I bask in joy, eternally free!

Queries in Chlorophyll

What do they think when I stand still?
Do they wonder if I'm heartless, or if I have a will?
I eavesdrop on gossip while sipping in light,
These silly humans think they're out of my sight.

Do they know about my secret plant chat?
The way I make jokes about their silly cat?
I'll keep their secrets, don't want them to fret,
But that bouncy little thing? Ah, I'll never forget.

Each dust speck's a mystery they can't comprehend,
While I bask here, my leafy, green friend.
When will they learn that I'm the true queen?
With roots in the soil, I rule this scene.

So, bring on the watering, I'm thirsty for more,
Perhaps I'll grow some new leaves and dance on the floor.
With every new sprout, my humor will thrive,
In this green jungle, I'm fabulously alive!

Moments in the Quiet

In stillness I ponder, they chat far away,
What's a geranium, without a bit of play?
When the sun hits just right, I bask in my seat,
Watching the world, as I wiggle my feet.

The dust on the shelf? It’s my homey abode,
I know all the secrets of this little road.
Oh, how I giggle at their uncanny slips,
Too busy they are to give me their tips.

A spider may dance, but I’m the real show,
With leaves that can sway, I simply steal the glow.
They wonder what I think, little do they know,
With every deep breath, my chuckles will flow.

So, here in my corner, I savor the calm,
As they rush through the day, I’m the leafy balm.
In their busy moments, I chuckle and cheer,
With my silent observations, they have nothing to fear!

Fragments of Flourish

Each leaf tells a tale, of sunshine and rain,
While I watch them scurry, in joy and in pain.
They claim I'm so quiet, just sitting on shelves,
But my thoughts are a whirlwind, just crowded with elves.

Do they ever wonder if I dream in the dark?
While they snooze, I'm plotting my fragrant remark.
A sprout here, a sway there—just trying to bloom,
I throw quite the party, to cheer up the room.

The feline parade? I’ve seen it all play,
As they dart and they pounce, oh what a display!
I giggle at chaos that fills up the space,
My roots like to quiver; I'm part of the race.

So come join the fun, in this light-filled domain,
For a plant’s vivid laughter flows freely like rain.
In every small flourish, a jest needs to surface,
In my leafy embrace, find your own little purpose!

Messages in the Breeze

With whispers of wind, I send little clues,
To remind them to laugh and kick off their shoes.
As I sway in the air, I send giggles like seeds,
To nurture their spirits, just like gentle weeds.

Oh, how they flounder, with watering can, nice,
Too much or too little? I just roll the dice.
I’m here in the corner, oh what a grand show,
In this realm of plants, it’s all a big fro.

A tilt to the left, a stretch to the right,
I pose like a model, in morning’s soft light.
In every frail petal, resides a grand scheme,
To lift their hearts higher—oh yes, that’s my dream.

So lend me your ear, let’s giggle a bit,
In my leafy embrace, life’s never a hit.
Together we’ll dance, let joy never cease,
For I'm here with my jokes, in the soft summer breeze!